POETRY FOR CHILDREN

The Land of Counterpane

By Robert Louis Stevenson
Illustrated by Nancy Harrison

The Child's World

Distributed by The Child's World®
1980 Lookout Drive • Mankato, MN 56003-1705
800-599-READ • www.childsworld.com

Acknowledgments
The Child's World®: Mary Berendes, Publishing Director
The Design Lab: Kathleen Petelinsek, Design

Library of Congress Cataloging-in-Publication Data
Stevenson, Robert Louis, 1850–1894.
  The land of counterpane / by Robert Louis Stevenson ;
illustrated by Nancy Harrison.
     p. cm.
  ISBN 978-1-60973-152-6 (library reinforced : alk. paper)
  I. Harrison, Nancy, 1963- ill. II. Title.
  PR5489.L36 2011
  821'.8—dc22   2011004998

Printed in the United States of America in Mankato, Minnesota.
July 2011
PA02091

When I was sick and lay a-bed,
I had two pillows at my head.

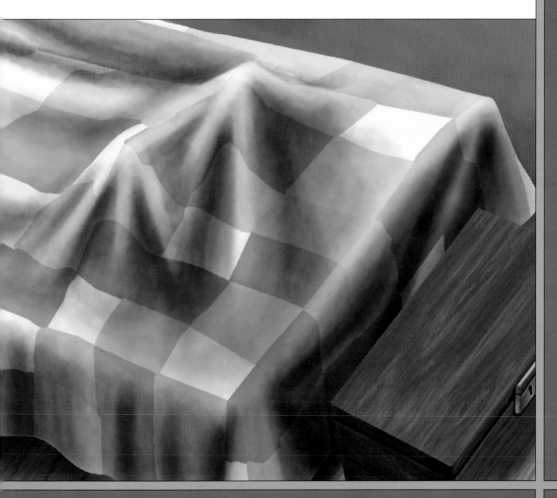

And all my toys beside me lay
to keep me happy all the day.

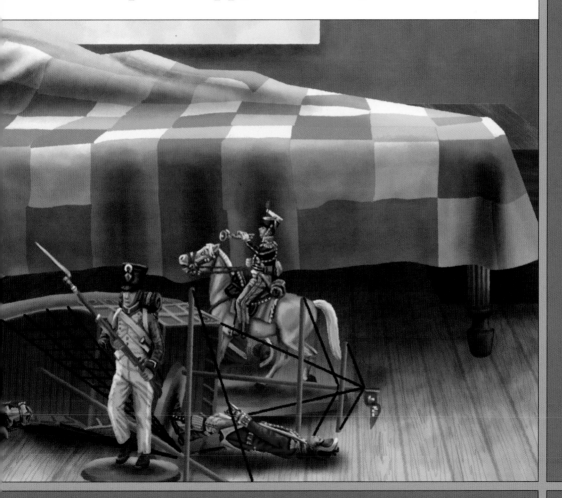

And sometimes for an hour or so
I watched my leaden soldiers go.

With different uniforms and drills,
among the bed-clothes, through the hills.

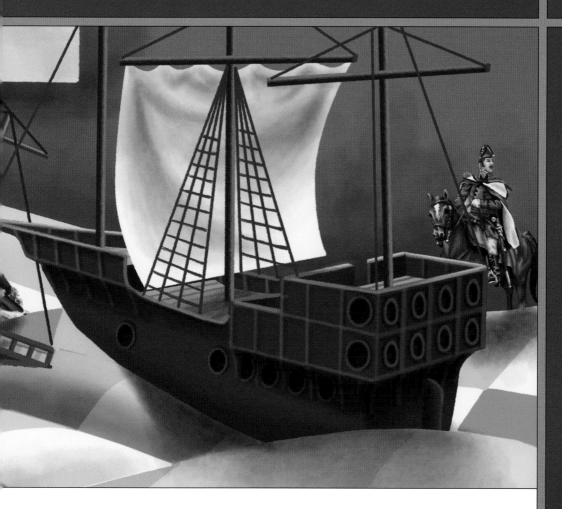

And sometimes sent my ships in fleets
all up and down among the sheets;

Or brought my trees and houses out ...